Key Stage 1

English
Revision Notes

Authors
Penny Coltman
Jayne Greenwood
Valerie Mitchell

Letts
EDUCATIONAL

The Authors and Publisher are grateful to the following for permission to reproduce copyright materials: page 58 © Meryl Domey from *The Very Worried Sparrow*, Lion Publishing plc.

First published 1999
Reprinted 1999
This edition 1999, 2000

Letts Educational,
9–15 Aldine Street, London W12 8AW
Tel. (020) 8740 2270
Fax. (020) 8740 2280

Editorial, design and production by Hart McLeod, Cambridge

British Library Cataloguing-in-Publication Data

A CIP record for this book is available from the British Library

ISBN 1 84085 326 3

Printed in Great Britain by Ashford Colour Press

CONTENTS

INTRODUCTION

Working through these revision notes will help your child to feel confident in English. They will also help you to understand some of the ways in which English is taught at Key Stage One.
The book is divided into clear sections, each dealing with a different area of English. In each section you will find:

- an explanation of the English skills covered
- ways in which you can help your child to learn and remember the skills
- activities which practise the skills.

Remember that little and often is the best recipe for success. Give plenty of praise and encouragement and remember that the golden rule is to stop when it becomes clear that your child has 'had enough'.

Working with words

PHONIC SKILLS

This section describes how you can help your child use phonic skills with their reading, writing and spelling.

Initial sounds

The ability to hear the initial sound in a word and match it with a letter is the first phonic skill that children need to learn.

How you can help

- Arrange sets of letters around the house. Magnetic letters on the refrigerator, sponge letters in the bath and alphabet books can act as starting points for letter recognition.
- Point out the initial letters on products around the supermarket. Make a short shopping list from pictures and words with the initial letter highlighted for your child to find.
- Play 'I spy' games at home to develop these skills and increase your child's confidence. Start with games that give quick success.

  Example Choose four objects with which your child is familiar, e.g. toys, clothes or food.
  Make sure they begin with different letters, *e.g. cup, pen, book, apple.*
  Arrange these articles on the table or tray and play 'I spy', e.g. *'I spy with my little eye something beginning with **p**.'*

  Keep the number of objects small at first and gradually increase the number.

- Play a variety of versions of this game, using different objects in different locations.

Letter touch

Make a collection of cut-out letter shapes. Make each letter several times out of different materials, *e.g. sandpaper, carpet, cotton, anaglypta wallpaper.*

Show your child how the letter is formed by tracing over it with your finger and then letting them copy. Put a green dot to show where to start and a red dot for where to stop.

Copy these letter shapes onto a piece of paper or into a scrap book for extra practice.

Letter pages

Look through a shopping catalogue together and find objects that begin with a chosen letter.

E.g. tricycle, trumpet, trousers, tin opener.

Cut out and stick around the letter **t** on paper.
Talk about the objects and repeat their names emphasising their initial sound.

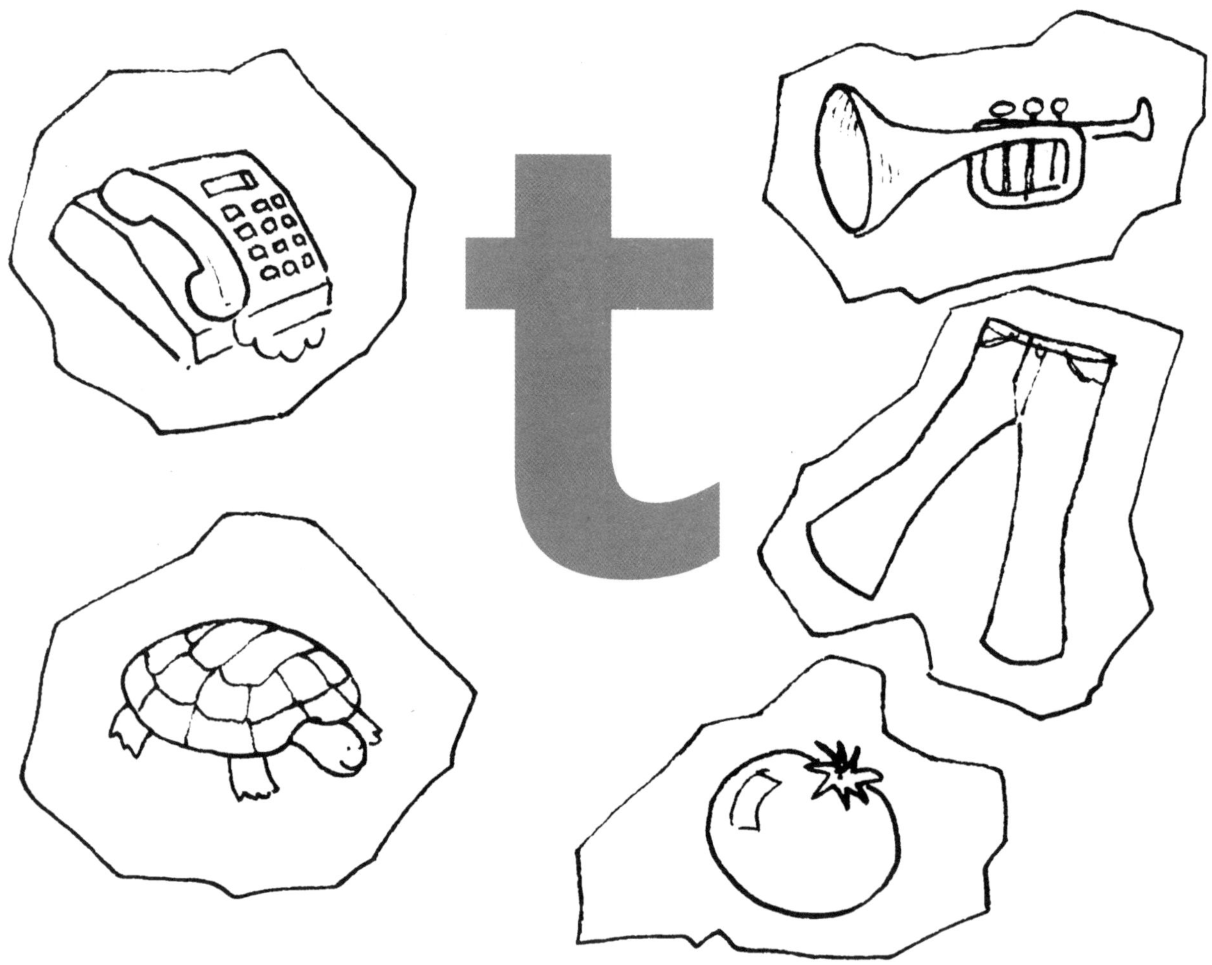

This activity can also be used for final sounds. Choose a letter to go in the middle of the page and then choose objects which end with that sound.

E.g. ***n****: pa****n****, pi****n****, bu****n.***

Word collections

Make a collection of words that begin with a chosen letter on the way to or from school.
As you walk or drive home, keep adding another word to your list.
Keep repeating the early words so that the sound is practised.

Examples **s**: **s**ign **s**ign **s**ky **s**ign **s**ky **s**treet
sign **s**ky **s**treet **s**ock **s**ign **s**ky **s**treet **s**ock **s**andwich

h: **h**ouse **h**ouse **h**over fly **h**ouse **h**over fly **h**ollyhocks

Thumbs up

Choose a letter sound.
Read a poem or rhyme and encourage your child to put their thumbs up every time they hear that sound.
To begin with, the poems or rhymes should be short with only a few of the sounds that you want to help your child identify.

Example **H h**
Humpty Dumpty sat on a wall,
Humpty Dumpty **h**ad a great fall
Hedgehogs and **H**ippos came **h**urrying by
And told **H**umpty off, for trying to fly!

*Thumbs up every time you hear the sound **h** in the poem.*

Alphabet journeys

Finding names of people and places that begin with the same sound can be fun. Try fitting these words into a sentence.
You could start with your child's name or at the beginning of the alphabet.
See how many you can get before you become stuck.

Example **A**lice and **A**lex went to **A**merica by **a**eroplane with **a**n **a**ardvark.
Fred and **F**elicity went to **F**rance by **f**erry with their **f**erret.

Final and middle sounds

When your child feels secure with the identification of initial sounds you can try the identification of middle and end sounds.

How you can help

- Play three different instruments: a drum, a shaker and a bell.
  Play them in different orders and ask your child to identify the first instrument, the last instrument or the middle instrument that played.
  This can help your child with the idea of sound sequencing.

- Help your child to identify the final sounds in words. Start with short, simple CVC (Consonant, vowel, consonant) words such as ha**t**, ca**t**, ca**p** or pa**n**.

Example Arrange a small collection of objects on a tray, a table or the bedroom floor.
Play 'I spy'.
'I spy with my little eye something ending with…'

Choose the toys or objects carefully for this game: avoid objects with very long names.
Keep the game short and successful.

Try to stop before your child loses interest, so that they look forward to the next time they play.

ACTIVITY

Alphabet Shopping

You could choose a friend's name and use this as a focus.

Example Mrs Flitting went shopping and only bought things ending with **m.**
Colour the things from this list which Mrs Flitting could buy?
E.g. ja**m**, ha**m**

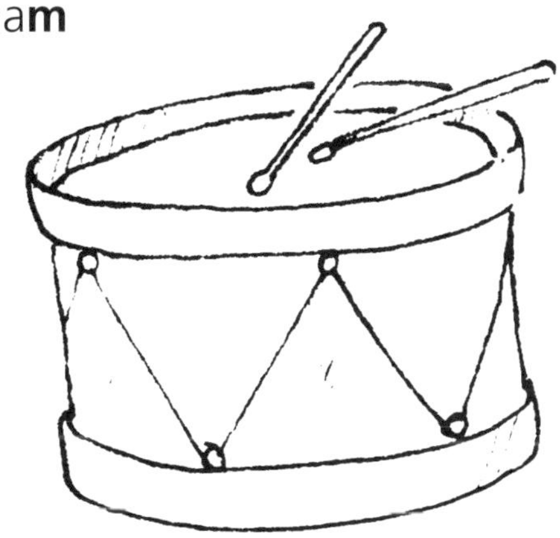

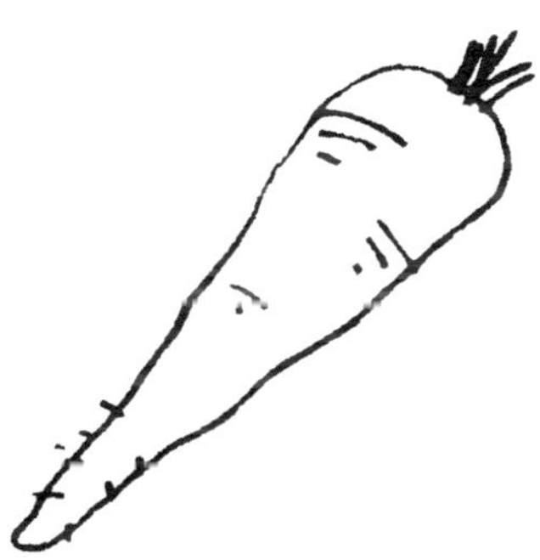

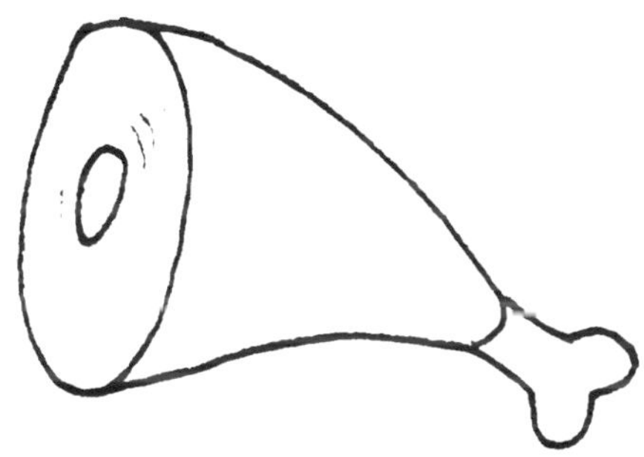

Make your own collection of items using other letters.

Word chains

Word chains help children with final sounds.

Here is a word chain:

cat top pen net toss shop pest train

Start with a simple word like cat. The next person has to give a word beginning with the final sound **t,** e.g. top. This activity identifies the final sound but your child has the simpler task of thinking up an initial sound word.

You can also write your word chains as steps.

cat
o
pen
e
toss
h
o
pest
r
a
i
n

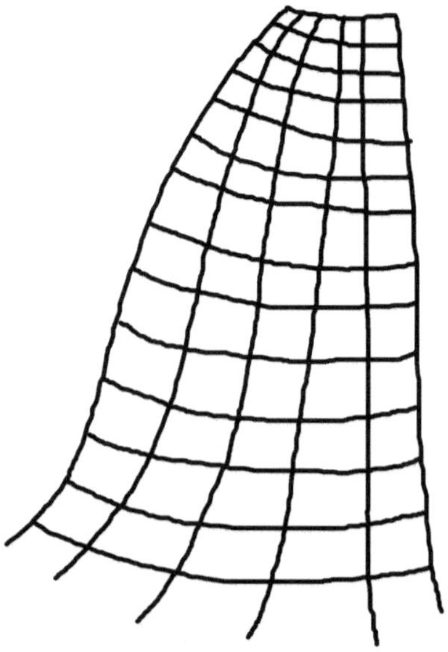

Find the middle letter

Make five cards like these, with the vowels **a e i o u**.

a e i

o u

Call out simple CVC (consonant, vowel, consonant) words and encourage your child to point to the card that shows the middle sound.

Suitable words:

c**a**t h**a**t m**a**t
h**e**n p**e**n f**e**n
p**i**n w**i**t f**i**t s**i**t
h**o**t c**o**t l**o**t
h**u**t b**u**t c**u**t

Phonic blends and digraphs

This section describes ways you can help your child to recognise, learn, and write blends and digraphs.

A blend

This is when two letters (consonants) are next to each other and although you can hear each letter sound, their sounds blend together.

Consonant blends:	**bl cl fl gl pl sl spl**
	br cr dr fr gr pr tr
	sc sk sm sp sn st scr spr str
	dw sw tw
Final consonant blends:	**-sk -sp -st**
	-ct -ft -lt -nt -pt -xt -lk -lm -lp
	-mp -nd -nk

A digraph

This is when two letters next to each other make a new sound and you cannot hear the two original letter sounds.

Consonant digraphs: **sh ch th wh ng ph tch dge**

How you can help

- Encourage your child to find words that begin with the same blends.
- Make up silly sentences for each blend.
- Write the sentences out with the blend written in another colour or highlighted.

  If you enjoy drawing cartoons try drawing an amusing cartoon to remind your child of the blend.

Examples

Black **bl**obs **bl**ow **bl**isters
Clever **cl**ams **cl**ean **cl**ogs
Flaming **fl**amingos **fl**ap **fl**ags
Lu**mp**s and bu**mp**s? Have you got mu**mp**s?

- Make a **blends band**.
  Cut out squares of card 5cm x 5cm. Write a blend or digraph on each square. With your child, draw a little picture of something beginning with each blend on the back of the letter blend card. Punch holes in the top left-hand corner of each square and thread these on to a piece of ribbon or tape.

  Do these a few at a time, no more than two or three a week.

  Play games with the blend band.
  Can you guess the sound this blend makes?
  If this is the picture, what is the blend?
  Find the two letters that make this blend.

- Play **Snip snap**

  You will need a set of blank cards. Old business cards or cards cut out of cereal packets are ideal.

  Choose five blends and write out a set of six word cards for each blend.

  Example **Ch**eck **ch**ick **ch**ip **ch**um **ch**ops **ch**ap
  flag **fl**ash **fl**an **fl**ip **fl**ing **fl**op
  brush **br**own **br**oom **br**other **br**im **br**anch
  thick **th**ump **th**ing **th**istle **th**imble **th**in
  skid **sk**etch **sk**ip **sk**unk **sk**ill **sk**in

  Play this game in the same way as playing card 'Snap'.
  Shuffle the cards and share them out equally.
  Each player places their cards down side by side at the same time.
  If the two word cards begin with the same blend, the first person to call 'snip snap' gets their opponent's cards.

- Play **Pick up pairs**

  Arrange the blend cards in rows. Players take turns to flip over two cards.
  If these cards have the same letter blend on them, the player may keep the pair and has another turn.
  If the words do not have the same letter blend, the player flips the cards back over and waits for their next turn.
  The winner is the player with the most matched pairs of blend cards.

Vowels

Knowing that vowels (the letters **a e i o u** and **y**) can say their name or their sound in a word can help your child with reading and spelling.

Vowels can have 'long' sounds or 'short' sounds.
Long sounds are the letter names (aay eey eye ow you). Short sounds are used when sounding out a word (ah eh ih oh uh).

How you can help

- Practise the vowels so that your child can say their names and their sounds.
- Think of a mnemonic to help them remember which letters are vowels.

  ***Y**oung **A**dam **E**ats **I**cy **O**nions **A**nd **U**nicorns*

- Explain the difference between the long and short vowel in words.

  short vowel sound .... c**a**t h**a**t fl**a**t
  long vowel sound .... st**a**ble m**a**ke fl**a**ke

  short vowel sound .... p**e**t m**e**t wh**e**n
  long vowel sound .... th**e**me **e**vil

  short vowel sound .... **i**nk p**i**ck
  long vowel sound .... l**i**ke b**i**cycle t**i**me

  short vowel sound .... c**o**t h**o**t **o**n
  long vowel sound .... g**o**at h**o**pe

  short vowel sound .... b**u**n **u**ntidy h**u**ng **u**mbrella
  long vowel sound .... **u**se **u**nit

- Explain that 'y' is often included with the vowels as it can represent three different vowel sounds.

  short 'i' sound .... h**y**mn g**y**m
  long 'i' sound .... sk**y** fl**y** wh**y** rh**y**me
  long 'e' sound .... cherr**y** quietl**y** merril**y**

- Study **tch or ch**

Knowing whether the vowel sound is long or short can help with spelling words that end in tch or ch.
If the vowel sound before the tch/ch sound is short use tch.
If it is long use ch.

Short vowels wre-**tch** ma-**tch** i-**tch**
Long vowels rea-**ch** tea-**ch** bee-**ch**

There are unfortunately some exceptions; **which, much, such, rich**

Write a collection of **tch** and **ch** words out and sort.

- **To double or not to double?**

Knowing about vowels can also help with how to sound out words ending with **ing**.

If there is a double letter the vowel has a short sound.
If there is a single letter after the vowel the vowel has a long sound.

si**tt**ing si**t**ing slo**pp**ing slo**p**ing ho**pp**ing ho**p**ing
swi**mm**ing sho**pp**ing se**tt**ing

Rhymes

Rhymes can help children decide which way to say a vowel when it occurs in a word. If two vowels are next to each other, in most cases the first vowel says its name and the second becomes silent.

A rhyme to help remember this is:

When two vowels go out walking
The first vowel always does the talking

Practise sounding out these words.

g**o**at b**o**at fl**o**at c**o**at r**o**ast

l**e**ad h**e**ad m**e**ad pl**e**ad

gr**e**ed f**e**ed w**e**ed n**e**ed

p**a**id l**a**id m**a**id r**a**id

l**i**e d**i**e

tr**a**in r**a**in n**a**il p**a**il s**a**il

r**o**ad l**o**ad t**o**ad

t**o**e h**o**e f**o**e

Names

The words below have either a short 'e' or long 'e' sound.
Encourage your child to sort these into two groups.
Say the words together so that it is easier for your child to hear the sounds.

Colour the short 'e' sounds in red
and the long 'e' sounds in blue.

pet	near	them
red	her	be
here	even	then
me	next	real
bed	she	were
these	over	there
help	we	

Magic 'e'

This section describes ways in which you can introduce and explain about magic or lazy 'e', to more experienced readers and those children who have noticed vowel sound changes for themselves.

How you can help

- Magic 'e' is where the **e** at the end of a word stays silent but makes the previous vowel into a long sound. An example of this is the word **hate**. If you take the word '**hat**' and sound it out each letter makes a short letter sound. If you add magic 'e' to make the word hate then the '**a**' becomes its letter name, a long sound 'aay'.
- Point out that there are other words where vowels sometimes say their names rather than their sound, e.g. baby.
- When talking about vowels take the opportunity to introduce the term consonant. Explain that the other 21 letters of the alphabet that are not vowels are called consonants.
- Using alphabet letter cards make some three letter words by placing a vowel between two consonants. Can you make a new word by adding a magic 'e' card to the end of your word? Suitable three letter words would be *pin, tub,* and *cap.*

Magic 'e'

Make a magic 'e' card like this.

Lay your magic 'e' card next to
each of the words below.
Can you read the new word?
Talk about the new sound that the first vowel in the word now makes.

bit	fir
pan	fin
can	win
rat	hop
mad	

Gather together as many magic 'e' words as you can find and write them out onto special cards to store in your collection.

ACTIVITY

Magic 'e' sentences

Make up silly sentences that use the pairs of words below.
Each pair has a word and its magic 'e' partner.

E.g. The man used branches from a **fir** tree to light a **fire**.

fir – fire

win – wine

hop – hope

scrap – scrape

slid – slide

Magic 'e' rhymes

Have fun making up rhyming magic 'e' pairs.

There once was a lady from Thake
Who wanted to ice a big ____________

There once was a vicar from Rome
Who wanted a church with a ____________

There once was a laddy called Mike,
Who escaped from his dad on his ____________

There once was an almighty gale
Which turned all the children quite ____________

There once was a kitten called Smee
Who got stuck in the top of a ____________

There once was a teacher, Miss Neat
Who gave all the children a ____________

ALPHABETICAL ORDER

This section describes ways of helping your child to learn the alphabet.

How you can help

- Practise saying the alphabet together.
  Breaking the alphabet down into smaller groups of letters and learning a little bit at a time can make the task easier.

  abcdefg hijklm nopq rstu vwxyz
  abcdefg hijk lmnop qrs tuv wxyz

- Learn the alphabet like a song. Ask your child's teacher the song that the school uses to teach the alphabet so that you can practise at home.

- Say the alphabet out loud and leave spaces for your child to fill in letters. This can help to ensure that your child feels they are succeeding.

- Start with small groups of letters with easy gaps.

  a__cdefg ab__defg abcdef__

  Let your child start the alphabet and you finish it: **abc** (child) **defg** (adult). As your child becomes more confident you can say alternate letters.

  b d f h j l n p r t v x z
  a c e g i k m o q s u w y

- Practise the middle sections with your child starting at different letters each time. Encourage your child to start at **g** and complete the next six letters or start at **w** and say the letters to **z.**

- Practise the whole alphabet in sections. You can add a clap or jump to reinforce the gap between each learnt section. This can give a little gap for thought.

  abcdefg clap **hijklmnop** clap **qrs** clap **tuv** clap **wx** clap **y and z** clap

- Do a little each day and always try to end with an activity that you know your child does well.

Magnetic letters

Carefully arrange a set of magnetic alphabet letters in order on the refrigerator door. Start by moving one letter out of order each morning, so that your child can find the one that is wrong as they eat their breakfast. Gradually start moving more around till they can all be muddled and your child is sufficiently confident to move them back into order.

Sponge Letters

If you have sponge letters, groups of letters could be stuck to the side of the bath for your child to organise into order.

Start with a different letter each time and when they are really good try going backwards from z! This skill can help in the future when your child uses a dictionary.

Make sure that they are the correct way round.

ACTIVITY

Animal alphabet

Make collections of alphabet animals.
Write their names in a scrap book and cut out or draw pictures of each one.
The library can be a good starting place for alphabet books.

Example **a**ardvark **b**adger **c**heetah **d**og **e**lephant **f**ox **g**oat

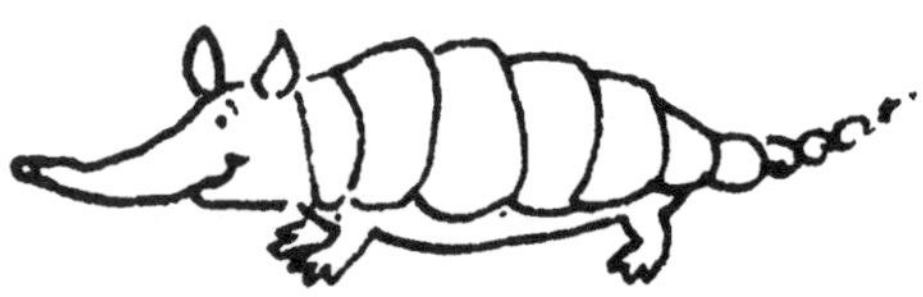

aardvark

badger

dog

elephant

cat

goat

fox

Alpha snakes

Which letters are missing?
Fill in the gaps in these Alpha snakes.

Try some of your own.

Making an address book

Buy a commercial address book or make one from an exercise book.
Talk about how you choose where to put people's addresses.
Does Granny go under G or under the first letter of her surname?

Don't try to fill the book in a day. Do one or two addresses every day for a week.

Using directories

When your child is confident with his own address book, try the challenge of the residential pages of a **telephone directory** to find school friends' or relations' telephone numbers.

Look at the way the **Yellow Pages** are arranged. Try finding your child's school telephone number together or the local sports leisure centre number.

Using dictionaries

The pages of dictionaries can be split into four sections:

A–E F–M N–S T–Z.

If you open a dictionary at the middle position you should find that you are in the section for letter **M**.
If your child is secure in her knowledge of the alphabet she should be able to predict which section to turn to first, second, third or fourth.

Try this out in practice to see how accurate it is.

READING FOR INFORMATION

This section describes ways in which you can help your child to find information from non-fiction books and other sources.
Many children will choose to read non-fiction books for pleasure and this should be encouraged.
It is important that the child is able to read the book easily in order to understand it.

How you can help

- When out and about encourage your child to read signs and notices, e.g. at the supermarket, garage, shops, library, station and school.
- Read packets and labels together, e.g. information on cereals, crisps, tins, bottles and packets.
- Work together to follow a set of instructions, e.g. making up a model, following a recipe, working with a construction set.
- Show your child how to read a television guide. Set simple problems such as asking the time at which a favourite programme begins.
- Read simple bus, train, ferry timetables together.
- Look at the different ways in which information is presented on tickets, leaflets, brochures, guides, newspapers, books.

- Encourage your child to read the children's section of the newspaper.
- Talk about the differences between fiction and non-fiction books. Make a point of reading non-fiction books sometimes at storytime/bedtime.
- Use information books together. Explain how the relevant section can be found by using a contents page.
- Show your child how an index page is arranged and how to look up a particular subject.
- If available, show your child how to obtain information from Teletext, Ceefax, the Internet or a CD Rom/Encyclopaedia.

Sorting fact from fiction

When your child understands the difference between fiction and non-fiction make a collection of story and information books, either the child's own or borrowed from the library.

Encourage your child to sort them into two piles and make a label for each type.

Look carefully at the pictures of books below and talk about whether they are story or information books. How do you know?

Using contents and indexes

Your child needs to know that a contents page gives a general heading with a page reference number.

The index page gives more specific subjects or words and also gives all the page numbers where these subjects are to be found.

Choose an information book that your child can read independently and read the contents page together. Take it in turns to ask each other questions about which page certain subjects can be found on.

Do the same using the index of the book. Check to see if there are actually references to the subject on the given pages.

Researching information

Read together the information on this cereal packet.

Use the questions below to give you ideas about the types of information your child can obtain from packets and labels.

Before what date is it best to eat this cereal?

How much does the packet weigh?

Which company made the cereal?

Does the company just want the cereal to be eaten at breakfast time?

Why do you think the company put a 'Best before' date on the packet?

SIGHT RECOGNITION WORDS

This section describes ways that you can help your child to learn words that cannot always be worked out using phonic skills.
You can help your child to read and write high frequency words such as colour words, number words, the days of the week and the months of the year.

How you can help

- Make collections of coloured objects.
  Start with a packet of crayons or coloured pencils.
  Let your child choose one coloured crayon/pencil and find things from around the house that match the colour.
- Take the opportunity to discuss the different shades of a colour that they find.
- Point out the houses that have written numbers on their doors or gates rather than numerals.
- Show your child that numeral words are used in story books rather than numeral figures.
- Make a collection of diaries and calendars and look at these together.
  Writing family birthdays on a new calendar can help children visualise how days and months are arranged.

- Cut the names of the days of the week out of an old calendar and put these in order.
  First start with Monday, then start with Tuesday
  It is important that children are aware of how the pattern keeps repeating so make sure that your child has opportunities to sequence two or three weeks.

- Use visual cues to reinforce the order of the months of the year.

  Example:

  JF
  MAM
  JJ
  A SON
  D

  This pattern can help children remember the order of the months.

- Help your child to say the months in order adding an action for each month.

Example:	January	Clap
	February	Turn around
	March	Hands on hips
	April	Hands on shoulders
	May	Hands on head

  These physical reminders can help your child to remember the sequence.

- Point out the rhymes that can help your child remember how many days there are in each month.

  Thirty days hath September,
  April, June and November.
  All the rest have thirty-one,
  Save February clear, with twenty-eight,
  And twenty-nine in each leap year.

- Play **Colour pairs**

  Play games with the words for colours.
  Start by writing the word for each colour in the appropriate coloured felt-tipped pen.
  Then write the words again in black.
  You can then play 'Find the pair'.
  Encourage your child to look carefully at the shape of each word and the letters to find the correct match.

red red

- Play **skipping games**

  These can combine physical activity with the ordering of numbers, days of the week or months of the year.

  One, two buckle my shoe,
  Three, four knock at the door,
  Five, six pick up sticks,
  Seven, eight lay them straight,
  Nine, ten a big, fat hen.

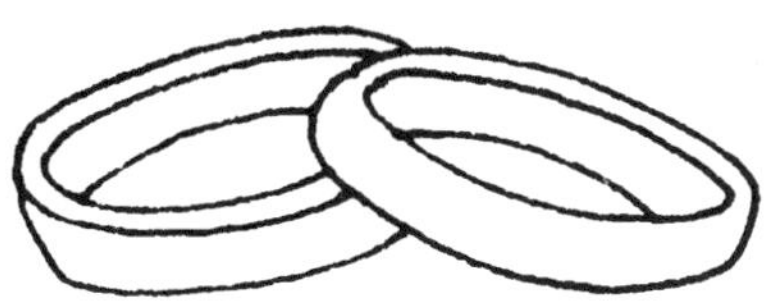

  Today I met my true love,
  My true love said to me,
  I'll marry you this week my dear,
  say what the day will be
  Monday? Tuesday? ... Sunday.

  My love's birthday
  When will it be?
  Turning rope,
  Please tell me.
  January?, February?, March? ... December.

- Read together **poems** about the days of the week and months of the year.

Months

January is the first
Really hope the pipes don't burst
February follows on
Winter snow may soon be gone
March brings yellow springtime flowers
Tulips bloom in April showers
In May the blossom starts to bud
In June the cows are chewing cud
July comes next, the days rush by
Holidays that seem to fly
August days are long and sunny
Bees are busy making honey
September sees the start of fall
Apple pies for one and all
October hedgehogs settle down
In fallen leaves of frosted brown
November fireworks split the skies
And high above a rocket flies
At last the year is nearly done
December brings us Christmas fun

Monday's child is fair of face,
Tuesday's child is full of grace,
Wednesday's child is full of woe,
Thursday's child has far to go,
Friday's child is loving and giving,
Saturday's child works hard for a living.
But the child that is born on the Sabbath day
Is bonny, blithe, good and gay.

Solomon Grundy
Born on a Monday
Christened on Tuesday
Married on Wednesday
Took ill on Thursday
Worse on Friday
Died on Saturday
Buried on Sunday
That was the end of Solomon Grundy.

ACTIVITY

Number jigsaws

Use simple number jigsaws to help your child learn number names.

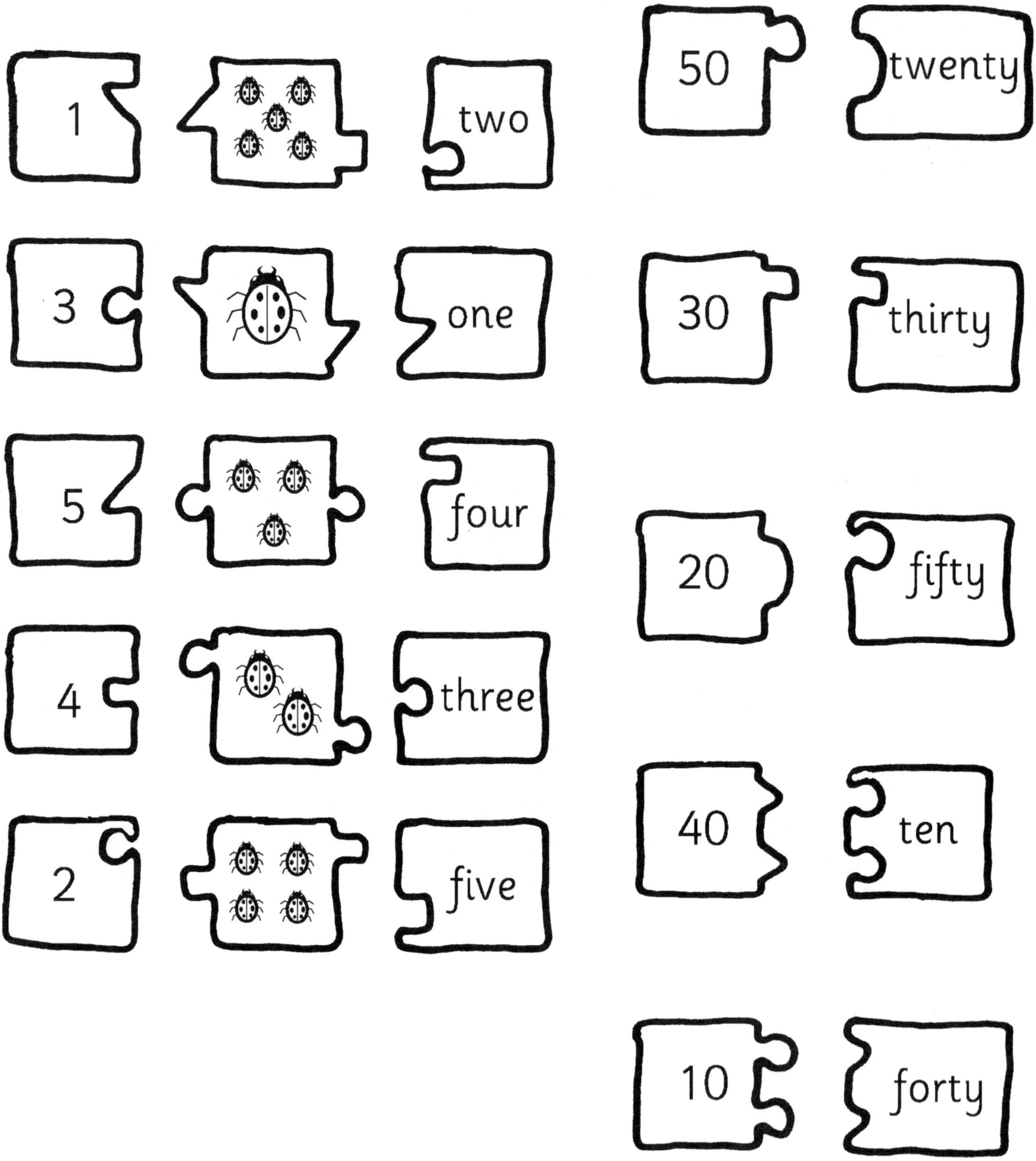

COMMON IRREGULAR WORDS

There are a lot of everyday words in the English language which do not fit into phonic patterns.
These are words that need to be learnt as sight words.
This section describes ways that you can help your child to learn these.

How you can help

- Reading a wide range of books allows your child to encounter these words in a variety of contexts.
  Try looking at fiction, non-fiction, plays, newspapers and comics, recipes and instruction booklets, even signs in supermarkets and on food labels.
- Play games such as 'Hunt and stab' and 'Happy families'.
- Use known and made up **mnemonics** to help your child remember the order of letters in words.

Examples	**said**	**S**illy **a**nts **i**n **d**ustbins
	because	**B**ig **e**lephants **c**an **a**lways **u**nderstand **s**mall **e**lephants
	what	**W**hat **h**as **A**lan **t**ickled?
	laugh	**L**augh **a**nd **u**se **g**ood **h**umour

- Use funny phrases to reinforce spelling patterns.

Examples	**island**	**Is land** surrounded by water?
	friend	My **Fri**day friend

  Think back to how you learnt these sorts of words. Most adults have a repertoire of tricks for remembering ways or ordering letters in irregular words.

- Have fun making some new ones for words you know your child finds hard.

  Look at the section of the word that is causing problems and think of a visual or rhyme clue that might help.

Example	T**ues**day	Under Ed's Shoe
	Th**urs**day	Under Rob's Shoe

Make up your own memory aids

- Play **Hunt and stab**

  Make a set of small cards with an irregular word written on each card once.
  Choose a group of six words. Arrange the words randomly on a tray or table. Call out a word and ask your child to hunt for it and point to it.
  If they get it right they keep the card.
  If they don't get it quite right then you take the card.
  Stop when all the cards are used.
  Choose different sets of words or different numbers of words for this game but always try to end on a successful game.

> *Try to ensure that your child wins more often than you do!*

- Play **Happy families**

  Some irregular words can be learnt by linking them to word families:

  e.g. *the/they* *other/brother/mother/another*

  All these words have the letter string 'the'.
  Linking them can help children to visualise family groups.

  Make Happy family cards:

Example	**the**	**ear**
	the y	**h ear**
	o the r	**h ear d**
	bro the r	**h ear ing**
	mo the r	**ear ring**
	ano the r	**t ear**

- Try making up phrases to reinforce these lists.
  e.g. *Where is it?* *There it is! No here it is!*

To, too, two

Draw a picture together to help your child remember these different spellings of to, too, two.

to splash

too many sweets

two swans

ACTIVITY

Mnemonic cards to copy

silly **a**nts **i**n **d**ustbins

said

big **e**lephants **c**an **a**lways **u**nderstand **s**mall **e**lephants

because

Is land surrounded by water?

island

A piece of pie

piece

Working with sentences

PUNCTUATION

A **sentence** is a group of words that make sense. It starts with a **capital letter** and ends with a **full stop**, a **question mark** or an **exclamation mark**. The sense may be made clearer by inserting **commas**.

This section describes how you can help your child to use punctuation to assist them to read fluently and write effectively.

Children need to know that good punctuation can help the reader to read and understand.

Children benefit from knowing when to use capital letters and full stops in their own written work and how to use commas to clarify lists.

How you can help

Capital letters

Familiarise your child with capital letters wherever possible, explaining when to use them in writing.

Capital letters are used for:

→ the beginning of sentences
→ people's names
→ place names
→ days of the week
→ months of the year
→ titles of books or plays
→ the pronoun 'I'

- Point out capital letters.

  E.g. *on packaging at the supermarket or on cereal packets at breakfast, on road signs and car registration plates, on timetables and calendars, at the start of names.*

- Help children to recognise capital letters, to say their names and the sounds they represent.

- Match lower case letters to capital letters. Magnetic letters often have both cases and can be put in pairs on the refrigerator.
- Encourage your child to match words that are the same where one begins with a capital letter.

  E.g. *The/the* *There/there*

Full stops

Emphasise the importance of full stops by reading a page from a reading book without putting in the pauses.

- Read the passage below without taking a breath.

  It was Gerald's birthday he was six he had an enormous party for all his friends they brought him lots of exciting presents Gerald was really happy.

  Make sure you sound out of breath by the time that you have finished.
  Ask your child what they think is missing.

- Explain that full stops help to make reading make sense by showing the reader where to pause.
  Read the above passage putting in the full stops. Ask which version sounded best or was easiest to understand.

Commas

Your child will need to know how to use commas when writing a list in a sentence.

- Point out commas in lists in your child's reading books and in TV Guides.
  E.g. *Jayne took a pencil, eraser, pen and note book to school.*
- Explain that commas are used to show small pauses in reading.
  They help to make the listed items clear to the reader or listener.

Spotting beginnings and endings

Show your child how to spot the capital letters and full stops in the story below.

Use two different coloured pens, one to highlight the capital letters and one to highlight the full stops.

Point out that the full stops are always followed by a capital letter but the capital letters do not all have a full stop in front of them.

It was Gerald's birthday. He was six. On Monday he had an enormous party for all his friends. They brought him lots of exciting presents. Gerald was really happy.

Writing names

Write out lists of friends' names for a party or special occasion card list. Write the capital letters in a special gold or felt pen so that they really stand out.

Try to include an adult's name which begins with Mr, Mrs or Miss to show that these also need capital letters.

Make a special sign for your child's bedroom door. Decorate the initial capital letter of his/her name.

Word Pairs

There	there	This	this
Here	here	Can	can
What	what	When	when
how	how	Why	why

Inserting commas

Some sentences need commas. Put the commas where they are needed in the circles.

I would like sausages ◯ bacon ◯ tomato and egg for tea.

I walk to school with Jane ◯ Sita ◯ Prem and Francis.

Chocolates ◯ peppermints ◯ barley sugar and jelly beans are Gran's favourite sweets.

For this recipe you will need flour ◯ sugar ◯ milk and cooking oil.

Once your child is confidently identifying where to put capital letters, commas and full stops you can introduce question marks.

Question marks

Question marks help your child to add variety and expression to their reading and writing.

- Talk about the sort of words that often start a question.
  E.g. **Who? What? Where? How? Why?**
- Explain that we ask questions when we want to find out something and that these sorts of sentences require an answer.
- Talk about what happens when you ask a question. Does your voice sound different when you ask or read a question?
- Play games that involve your child thinking up a question.
- Play **Here is the answer, what was the question?**

  Think up a variety of answers to questions.
  Offer the answers and encourage your child to think what the question might have been.

Example	*Parent*:	*Child*:
	My name is Pete.	What is your name?
	I live in London.	Where do you live?
	I am seven.	How old are you?

Exclamation marks

Exclamation marks also assist reading and writing with expression.

- Demonstrate how they are used to indicate that a sentence should be read with great emotion such as anger, surprise, pain or amusement.

  E.g. *Help!* *Stop!* *Don't do that!* *Good heavens!*

- Collect !! words.

  E.g. *Stop!* *No!* *Wow!* *Danger!*

- Make signs to go up around the house.

  E.g. *Mind the step!* *'Beware of the dog/cat!'*

- Carry out a **Book search**

  Make a collection of sentences from your child's reading book of questions and exclamations.

  Use different colours for the different marks when you are writing them out.

Questions	**Exclamations**
Can you tell me the way to the farm?	Help!

VERBS AND ADVERBS

A **verb** is a word that tells you what somebody or something is doing or being.
An **adverb** tells you more about the verb.

How you can help

- Encourage your child to talk about what they are doing to find lots of verbs.
  The garden is a good place to try some of these.

  Examples I am **running** out to play.
  I am **hopping** round the garden.
  I am **skipping** up the path.
  I am **crawling** over the grass.
  I am **jumping** over the flower pot.

  These verbs describe what someone is doing.

- Explain that adverbs tell you something more about the verb.

  Examples I am running **quickly.**
  I am hopping **slowly.**
  I am skipping **carefully.**
  I am crawling **awkwardly.**
  I am jumping **fast.**

- Have fun discovering adverbs to describe a verb such as eating or walking.

  Examples I am walking **slowly.**
  I am walking **noisily.**
  I am walking **crossly.**
  I am walking **happily.**

Tenses past, present or future?

In reading and writing we use the past, present and future **tenses** of each verb to show when the action happened. Whether it was yesterday, today or tomorrow.

- Using the idea of yesterday, today and tomorrow makes understanding tense easier.

  Examples Yesterday I **played** in the garden.
  Today I **am playing** in the garden.
  Tomorrow I **will play** in the garden.

- Explain that sometimes the ending of the word changes and sometimes another word is added.
  The verb is the base word, e.g. to play, to run, to jump, to crawl.

- A common way of changing a verb into the **past tense** is to add **ed** to the base word. Find examples that fit this pattern.

Examples	play	play**ed**
	skip	skipp**ed**
	crawl	crawl**ed**
	jump	jump**ed**

- Some verbs use the ending **ing** to show the **present tense**. Find examples.

  Examples I am wait**ing**.
  I am cry**ing**.
  I am laugh**ing**.

- Some verbs change completely depending on the tense. Make a list of these and learn them together.

Examples	I **am**	I **was**	I **will be**
	I **went**	I **am going**	I **will go**

ACTIVITY

Describing play scenarios

Look at the action scene below.
Talk about the people and animals doing different things.
Colour the picture while you talk.

Examples Who is running?
Who is building?
Who is mending the car?
What is this man doing?
Which cars are crashing?
Which cars are parking?

Discuss books

Look at action books together.

E.g. *Where's Wally?* *The Cross Section books.*

Write lists

Make a list of things you did yesterday and things you are doing today.

Examples	Yesterday:	Today:
	I **played** with Joseph.	I **am playing** with Inez.
	I **went** to the library.	I **am going** to the park.
	I **jumped** over the hoops.	I **am jumping** over the skittles.

Find the endings

Take a theme and see how many verbs you can link to your theme.

Water

Root words:

to water	watering	watered
to flow	flow _ _ _	flowed
to pour	pouring	pour _ _
to drip	dripp _ _ _	dripped
to splash	splash _ _ _	splash _ _
to soak	soaking	_ _ _ _ ed

Working with texts

PLANNING A STORY

For children to be successful writers they have to have ideas on which to draw. A good way to model story ideas and conventions is to read stories regularly to your child and to talk about how the author makes you want to read on to find out what happens.

How you can help

- Discuss how a simple story is structured into a beginning, middle and end. A story usually **begins** by introducing the characters and places them in a setting. Quite near the beginning something usually happens that causes a problem, e.g. a teddy is lost or a child is frightened by something.
  The **middle** part of the story often deals with how the characters set out to resolve the problem.
  The **ending** is how things worked out for everyone.
- Read a favourite story to your child and at the end try to break it down into main events or stages.
  There may be more than the three stages suggested but try to keep any retelling to a very simple form.
- Work together to represent these main stages by drawing the ideas in boxes so that you end up with a type of cartoon retelling of the story.
- Reinforce story structure and planning by cutting a series of pictures that tell a story out of a comic or magazine, and playing a sequencing game.
- The emphasis at this stage should be on story-telling and building a bank of imaginative ideas rather than writing the stories down.

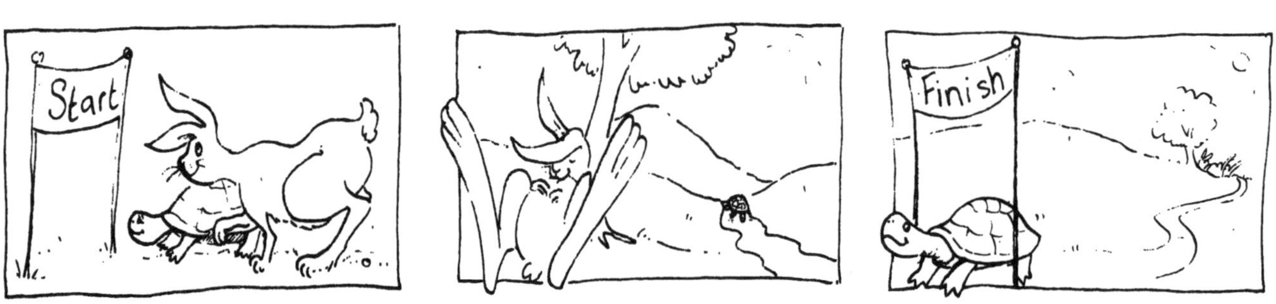

Finish the story

Read together the story below. It has a beginning section and a middle. When you have read the story make up an ending either by telling the rest of the story or writing it down.

Ben was looking for Teddy. He had hunted in all the places he usually left him, under the kitchen table, next to his bed, on the sofa, but he was nowhere to be seen. Ben was getting worried that bed time was not too far away. Soon his mum would be running his bath and asking him to put his pyjamas to warm on the radiator.

Now he was all ready for bed. Ben's mum told him not to worry. 'Teddy will soon show up,' she said. 'In the meantime take Rabbit to bed instead.'

Ben was not happy about this. Teddy had a lovely smell about him that kept silly dreams away. Ben cuddled up to Rabbit and tried to pretend that he was Teddy but it didn't work....

ACTIVITY

Drawing a beginning, middle and end

Read this story together and draw three pictures to show what the main parts of the plan would be.

One day Little Red Riding Hood went for a walk through the woods to visit her Grandma. Grandma had been ill and so Little Red Riding Hood had made her some chocolate cakes and was carrying them in a basket.

On the way through the woods Little Red Riding Hood met a wolf. The wolf was very kind and friendly. He asked her where she was going and offered to carry the heavy basket on ahead for her. He then said that he hoped her Grandma would soon be well. They said good-bye and Little Red Riding Hood went on her way.

When she arrived at her Grandma's cottage Little Red Riding Hood called to her Grandma to tell her that she had arrived. Grandma had been asleep in the chair and had not been expecting any visitors. Imagine how surprised they both were when they discovered that tea was already set out on the table with delicious chocolate cakes.

Writing a beginning, middle and end

Look carefully at the plan in the boxes below and write the story that you think was meant to happen.

beginning

middle

end

STORY COMPREHENSION

This section describes ways of helping your child with story comprehension skills. It is important that your child selects suitable books to read independently if they are to fully understand the story.

How you can help

- Encourage your child to choose a text where they can confidently read every word without a struggle. It does not matter if the book appears to be too easy for the child.

  Without understanding what they are reading there will be little enjoyment. This applies to non-fiction books as well as stories. Finding information without really understanding the text will prove extremely difficult.

- Talk about any difficult words that you have noticed so that your child reads them successfully when they come to them.

- When reading books together ask questions such as *'Who are the main characters in this story?' 'What happened first' 'Where is this story set?' 'Have you ever been anywhere like that?'*

- When part way through a shared story stop and ask your child to predict what they think might happen at the end.

- After reading a book together ask your child to retell or order the story in their own words.

- As children progress they will be able to answer questions about the story that are not always obviously stated but can be worked out. Examples of this type of question would be *'How do you know he is thinking that?' 'Do you think she is happy?'*

Jack and the Beanstalk

This story is muddled up. Read together the three parts of the story and talk about which order they should be in.

When Jack woke up the next morning his bedroom seemed to be very dark. As he looked out of the window he saw that a huge beanstalk had grown up during the night. The stem was so thick and the leaves of the plant so big that light was blocked from the room. Jack decided that he just had to climb the beanstalk to see what might be at the top...

There was once a boy named Jack. He lived in a cottage in the country with his mother. They were very poor and often did not have enough food to eat. One day when they were down to their last slice of bread, Jack's mother told him to take their only cow to market to sell.

On the way to market Jack met a man who bought the cow from him. The man gave Jack some magic beans instead of money and Jack was very pleased. When he got home his mother was not at all pleased. She shouted, stamped her foot and sent Jack to bed without any supper. She threw the magic beans out of Jack's bedroom window.

Answering questions

Read together the passage below.

There was once a Very Worried Sparrow. All the other birds looked up at the bright blue sky and sang for joy. But the Very Worried Sparrow hung his head, shut his beak tight and looked worried.
He had always worried, even when he was just a baby bird in the nest. His brothers and sisters kept saying, 'Cheep, cheep, cheer up!'
But the Very Worried Sparrow only said, 'Meep, meep, oh dear!'

Ask questions about the passage. The answers can be given verbally at this stage.

Some examples of questions to ask are:

What did the Very Worried Sparrow do that showed he was worried?
Had he always been worried?
What did his brothers and sisters say to him?
What did the Very Worried Sparrow say to his brothers and sisters?

Find the missing words

Read together the poem below.

Copy out the sentences beneath the passage and fill in the missing words.

My kitty-cat has nine lives,
Yes, nine long lives has she –
Three to spend in eating,
Three to spend in sleeping
And three to spend up in the
chestnut tree.

(Anon)

My kitty – ________________ has nine lives,

Yes, nine long lives has ________________ –

Three to spend in eating,

Three to ________________ in sleeping

And ________________ to spend up in the

chestnut tree.

LETTER WRITING

This section describes ways of helping your child to learn to write a letter. Letter writing is one of the many ways in which young children can find a purposeful context in which to use their writing skills.

How you can help

- Familiarise your child with his/her full name.
  Many children are able to write their first name well but are unsure about their surname.
- Talk about titles such as Mr, Mrs, Miss, Master and what they mean.
- Learn to set out an address. After the name the next line usually has the house number or name and street name. Next comes the village, town or area, then the city or district and finally the county and post code.
- Talk about the ways in which these details help the postman/woman to deliver the mail.
  Work together to write the child's own address.
- Talk about ways of writing the date; fully in words and the shortened way just using numbers.
- Look at how letters begin with *Dear* and point out the importance of beginning both this word, and the name of the person you are writing to, with capital letters.
- Encourage children to begin their letter underneath the comma after the name and to write in one long paragraph.
  Organising the various subjects of their letter into different paragraphs is too difficult at this stage.
- Children also need to know about the different ways of ending a letter. Look at how business letters are ended and then talk about more informal ways to use when writing to someone we know well.

ACTIVITY

Writing their own address

After looking at various addresses and how the information on each line is set out, your child will be ready to have a go at writing their own address.

Making a template by copying out the one below will reinforce, remind and support your child in the early stages of learning to set out their address correctly.

Name ....

House number or name & street ....

....

Village, town or area ....

City or district ....

County & postcode ....

Post games

To reinforce children's understanding of how letters are addressed, encourage your child to act as 'post person'.
This could involve collecting up the mail and sorting it into piles for the various people in the household.
They can then be responsible for 'delivering' it to each individual.

Encourage your child to send themselves (and possibly others in the household) a postcard.
This will provide a real situation for writing their own address, setting out a message and talking about why post has to have a stamp.
When it arrives talk about what is different about it.

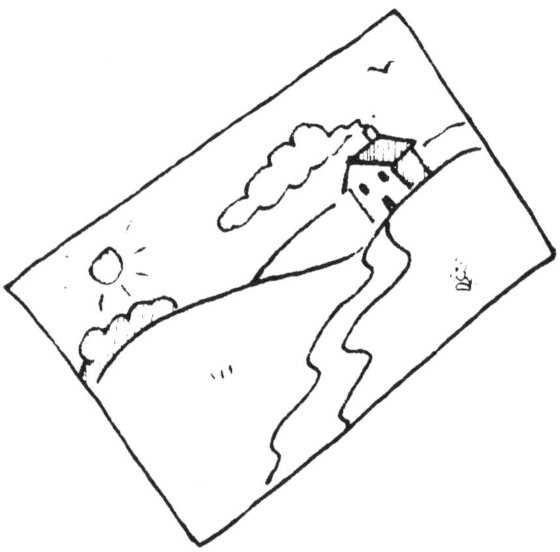

More addresses

Now try writing other people's addresses for extra practice.
Written below are the lines of an address which need sorting into the correct order.

Look carefully before you write to see which line goes where.

3 Toy Street,
Play City
Teddyshire
TB10 1NS
Teddy Bear
Toy Village.

HANDWRITING

This section describes how you can help your child with skills that will develop their fine motor control.
These skills will support their handwriting.

How you can help.

- Play games that involve moving small counters around a board.
- Show your child how to make patterns with coloured pegs which fit into a peg board.
- Let your child have fun popping plastic bubble wrap using just the finger and thumb of their writing hand. How many can they pop in 30 seconds?
- Make small models out of plasticine.
- Thread large wooden beads onto shoe laces.
- Paint pictures using a variety of brush sizes.

Letter formation

Letters can be grouped according to how they are formed.

iltjf *Group 1*

ecoadgqs *Group 2*

rnmh *Group 3*

bkp *Group 3a*

vwuy *Group 4*

zx

Group 1 is made up from the letters that need a straight vertical line.
Group 2 is made up from the letters that start with a c shape.
Group 3 is made up from the letters that start with an overwritten vertical line.
Group 3a starts the same way as group 3 but then need a loop of some sort.
Group 4 start with a down stroke followed by an angled up stroke.
Z and X need to be learnt separately.

ACTIVITY

Peg board fun

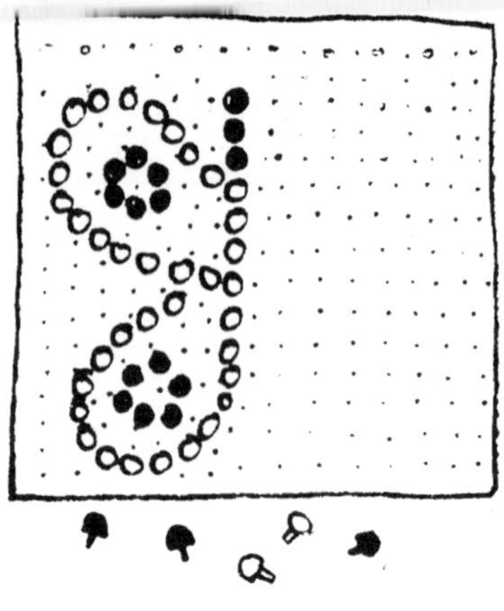

You will need a peg board with a selection of different coloured pegs. Using coloured pegs, fill in half of a pattern on one side of the board. Show your child how to copy then repeat the pattern on the opposite side using the coloured pegs.

This activity helps with the vertical up and down movement needed for Group 1 letters

---

Make your own marbles

Using salt dough mix, encourage your child to make small balls of dough, using their index finger to roll the mixture. Bake these in the oven till hard and then decorate with paint or felt-tipped pen. They can then be varnished to add an extra protective layer.

This activity helps your child with the circular movement needed for Group 2 letters.

Clapping games

Games that involve clapping hands with a partner or slapping thighs can help with the movements for Group 3 letters.

Clap hands, stand up and slap your thighs
Point your fingers to the skies
Bring them down
Then stretch them out
Flap your arms and then you're out

Sweetie pick up

Arrange a selection of small regular shaped sweets on a saucer. Show your child how to suck through a drinking straw and pick each sweet up individually and put it in a cup or mug. Challenge them to see how many they can do in 20 seconds.

This activity can help with the zig-zag pattern needed for Group 4 letters.